# Comanche Cafe
## and
# Domino Courts

*By William Hauptman*

SAMUEL FRENCH, INC.

45 WEST 25TH STREET      NEW YORK 10010

7623 SUNSET BOULEVARD      HOLLYWOOD 90046

LONDON      TORONTO

COMANCHE CAFE was first produced professionally by Wynn Handman and Julia Miles at the American Place Theatre in November, 1976; under the direction of Barnet Kellman; with the following cast:

RONNIE .................... *Jane Galloway*

MATTIE ................ *Sasha von Scherler*

Set design by Henry Millman; lighting design by Eddie Greenberg; costumes by Carol Oditz; production stage manager, Richard S. Viola.

# Comanche Cafe

*A near-empty stage.* RONNIE, *an attractive girl in her mid-twenties, stands* C.S. *staring out. There are two chairs* D.L. MATTIE, *an overweight woman in her forties, sits in one of them. There is a bucket of potatoes beside the chairs. During the play, both women peel potatoes.* MATTIE *sometimes reads the paper.*

*Behind them is a bright expanse of sky and a distant line of telephone poles.* U.S. *of them and right are many small plaster statues like those seen for sale in front of gas stations and cafes on country roads—dogs, rabbits, ducks, and Dutchboys. The set represents the Comanche Cafe, a roadside diner somewhere in Southern Oklahoma in the late Nineteen-Thirties. Gospel music is heard on a radio, fading out as the lights come up.*

RONNIE. I don't see why we've got to work on Sunday.

MATTIE. Why not?

RONNIE. I'd rather not spend my Sundays peeling potatoes out in back of the Comanche Cafe.

MATTIE. I like working on Sundays. It's not much good for anything else.

RONNIE. You got a lot of customers here. We never had so many at the Selpa Diner. But you're on the main highway. Seems like the whole country's on the move. Everybody's leaving Oklahoma. It's this wind. Sometimes I think it's going to blow the whole town away. (*Pause.*) What else do I have to do?

MATTIE. Fold napkins, wash tablecloths, and mop the floors.

RONNIE. And we always have to peel potatoes?

MATTIE. On days when the cook's too busy.

RONNIE. We never had to at the Selpa Diner.

MATTIE. This isn't the Selpa Diner. It's a small operation. Everybody's got to pitch in.

RONNIE. How long have you worked here?

MATTIE. Fourteen years.

RONNIE. Fourteen years. That's a lot of spuds.

MATTIE. It's your first day on the job. You'll learn to like it. You get to meet all sorts of people here.

RONNIE. Like who?

MATTIE. In the morning you get the truckdriving boys. They're my favorites. They come in here with their arms sunburned and they like their coffee and pie. In the afternoons you get the salesmen. You'll know them by their two-toned shoes and celluloid collars and dirty jokes. And in the evenings you get the farmers. They're mostly worn-out men wearing overalls. They order coffee and their meal's a toothpick. (*She reads the paper.*)

RONNIE. . . . Wonder what's going to happen to me here. Maybe I'll meet a man. Those truckdriving boys sounded nice. (MATTIE *laughs*) What?

MATTIE. Says here some woman in Tulsa took a snapshot of God with a Kodak Brownie.

RONNIE. I don't believe in God. Ghosts, that's what I believe in. Things are going on underneath all this, Mattie, unbelievable things.

MATTIE. Bull.

RONNIE. What's more, I can foretell the future. Premonitions they're called. I always know if the water's going to boil or when the sun's about to come out from behind a cloud. And the other day I knew THE SHADOW was going to be on before I ever touched the radio. No, I don't believe there's a God. But somebody told me once God was a fat woman. She lives in a trailer down in Florida with her cats and watches the sun go down. . . .

MATTIE. (*Alertly.*) What are you getting at?

RONNIE. Nothing. It's just something somebody told me once, that's all. You ever want to travel, Mattie?

MATTIE. What for? Everyplace is the same.

RONNIE. Every one of these cafes is the same. The stools, the counter. Those old cakes on the counter under those glass domes. If I can only get out of here—then anything's possible. Maybe I'll go to California and break into movies.

MATTIE. Fat chance.

RONNIE. Lots of people have told me I could make my living on my looks. How am I going to know they're wrong if I don't try?

MATTIE. There's nothing out there. No matter where you go, you always find out nothing looks like the postcard. You go to Hourglass Lake, but the postcard doesn't show you how gray the water is, or how dirty the sand. The postcard leaves too much out.

RONNIE. Not if you're in love. Then you don't notice the dirt. You ever been in love, Mattie?

MATTIE. Nope, I've been a waitress for fourteen years.

RONNIE. I've got to fall in love. Catch a man who'll take me out of here so I don't have to work.

MATTIE. I'll stay here at the Comanche Cafe. Without work, everyday's a day off—and everybody knows Sunday's the worst day of the week.

RONNIE. I feel sorry for you, Mattie. You're going to let life pass you by. There's lots of men coming in here every day. I don't know why you haven't caught one. 'Course . . . I guess somebody like you isn't interested.

MATTIE. Why not?

RONNIE. Well . . . you don't look like you would be.

MATTIE. Let your hair down.

RONNIE. Don't worry, it's not too late to the find the right man.

MATTIE. I'm not looking.

RONNIE. I understand. And in a way I envy you—you've never been in love, but you've never known the pain of losing someone. But anything's possible. (*Pause.*) Even for a fat woman.

MATTIE. So. You don't think a woman like me can get a man? I had a man come in here once who asked me to run away with him.

RONNIE. I thought you'd never been in love.

MATTIE. This wasn't love. It was something else. He came in here one Spring, a sort of pasty-faced boy wearing a black hat. I'm so big I make most men feel like Charlie Chaplin. He looked like him, but he wasn't afraid of me. He had a Kodak Brownie, too, and all the time he was eating he kept looking at me with these sad, dark eyes. I said, you must like our cooking, and he wanted to know if he could take my picture because he said I had a beautiful smile.

RONNIE. So?

MATTIE. So I let him. They developed it at the drugstore and he brought it back the next day and showed it to me. Right then he said he wanted me to go away with him. He was short, but he had a way with words.

RONNIE. I told you: anything's possible.

MATTIE. I pinned up a note in the kitchen that night and we left first thing in the morning. I thought it was what I'd wanted to hear a man ask me almost my whole life. If he'd said let's go to a tourist court and back I would have laughed; but when someone asks you to go all the way to God knows where—well, who wouldn't go, that's the question. But in the end...I came back to the Comanche Cafe.

RONNIE. . . . Why?

MATTIE. You're young. You wouldn't understand.

RONNIE. (*Hotly.*) I'm not so young I don't understand a lot!

MATTIE. You never had a man, did you? (*Pause.*) Not yet.

RONNIE. No. I never had a man yet; not in bed, if that's what you mean. There have been boys, sometimes. But I always lost my nerve. Or they did. I guess you have. . . . (MATTIE *nods.*)

MATTIE. You don't know everything yet.

RONNIE. I know chances shouldn't be wasted. And when I find the man I want, I'll go after him and I'll do it right. You lost him, didn't you? This boy with the Kodak?

MATTIE. Yes. I lost him.

RONNIE. You did something wrong. I wouldn't have lost him—not if I really wanted him. Maybe I've never had a man, but I already know a lot about them.

MATTIE. How?

RONNIE. From the movies.

MATTIE. Movies aren't like real life.

RONNIE. Sure, they're not real, but men go for them, too, so what's the difference. Oh, but Mattie—Mattie— tell me. What's it like? Don't tell me how you lost him. But I've got to know what it's like to have a man, it's such a mystery to me. Is it beautiful? (*Pause.*)

MATTIE. 'Course it's beautiful. (*She tells the story slowly, mysteriously.*) When we started driving that morning I thought, now I'm going to see all the things I've heard about. I never thought it could happen to me. I didn't know where we were going, but I didn't care. That first night we stopped at a tourist court down in Texas. I remember everything about it—how he hung his pants on the back of a chair to save the crease. How the walls were thin as pasteboard. He put his watch on the dresser and his hair was combed with water. He came toward me and touched my shoulder. I was shaking and trying not to show it . . . And then, afterwards, we lay together. He smoked and told me the story of his whole life, and I could just see his face in the matchlight. Through the window there were a few stars scattered in the sky, like thumbtacks, and I remember that night there was a new moon and it looked like a piece of broken saucer... 'Course it's beautiful. (*Pause.*)

RONNIE. Sometimes I think I can't wait until it happens to me. Sometimes I think I'll throw myself at the next man who walks into this cafe.

MATTIE. When we got up the next morning, he took my picture standing in front of the car. I've still got it. But then we drove down to Fort Worth, and the romance began to fade. I began to wonder what I was doing there, and if there wasn't more to it than this— just being on the loose. Being free. In the end I bought a bus ticket and came back to work. I got here on a Monday morning.

RONNIE. But . . . why?

MATTIE. I found out I'm not made for love—I'm made for work.

RONNIE. Well, I'm not.

MATTIE. Look at me. (*Pause.*) You're looking for something. You think now it's a man. But it's something inside you—your ghosts. You're still young. But one day everything's happened. Then the night's no different from the day.

RONNIE. You could still find the right one. But anything's possible.

MATTIE. Even for a fat woman? Sure—I could always go to New York and become an opera singer. Wear pearls around my neck.

RONNIE. But every woman needs a man. It's something no woman can live good without.

MATTIE. This woman can.

RONNIE. You've got to get out of here, Mattie!

MATTIE. Don't feel sorry for me! (*Pause.*) That's how I felt about him. He was always smiling so serious and saying it could go on forever. I was always wear-

ing my best clothes, my scratchy gabardines. I couldn't
get comfortable. I kept trying to smile back but I was
holding my breath like I was about to hear a sermon.
Sometimes I looked at my picture to remind myself
how happy I was. There I stood, holding my new purse
and smiling. Everything was covered with dew and
the sunlight was shining down through the boughs of
the trees so you could see it like pencils on the air,
shining pencils. Oh, it looked nice—in the picture. But
I knew I couldn't go smiling through the rest of my
life with a nice little Charlie Chaplin. Now—I got a
bed, and a sink, and a chair, and a window. What
more do I need? Everyplace is the same.

RONNIE. No.

MATTIE. And so is everybody.

RONNIE. I'll never be like you. (*Pause.*) There's a
whole mysterious country out there, Mattie, and I'm
going to see it all. As soon as I can, I'm leaving. I'm
going to see Chicago and New York—the big cities up
North where everybody stays up all night long drinking black coffee. Life's more serious up there. I've
heard those all-night programs where people phone
in and talk about their problems. They've got a lot of
serious problems up there, that's all I've got to say. I
want to see Grand Central Station, the crossroads of
America, and the tallest buildings in the world. Sky-
writing floating on the clouds above the buildings all
day long. See Tin Pan Alley and Times Square and
newsboys everywhere you look and gangsters and
baseball players. People talk in newspaper headlines.
Everyplace is going out of business, and everybody
can be bought. Or I might go to California, where the
sun's always hot and you can see the movie stars walk
into the drugstore and buy aspirin just like normal
people. I might go there—I might—there's orange
groves and private eyes, and they say it never rains.
Or I might go down South, where people burn crosses

on the lawns, and hide their idiot sons in the attic. To Florida, where the hotels look like big white wedding cakes, and millionaires drive down the boulevards with the top down, smoking cigars. Moonlight and palm trees and waterspouts! Things I never saw before! Or I might even go to Georgia, where nobody ever goes. To the mountains, where it's always raining cats and dogs, and the hillbillies play their fiddles and drink moonshine. They marry down there when they're eleven years old. You don't know what you might do down there! The rain pours down and there's a house I heard about where there's no more law of gravity and water runs uphill. Wonderful things! Wonderful things all over America! And I'm going to see them all. Just let me be anyplace but here—in Oklahoma. (*Opera has been heard as she speaks, rising in volume. As she finishes, it reaches a finale. The stage darkens.*)

## PROPERTY PLOT

2 bentwood chairs
Several small plaster statues like those seen for sale in f
   of gas stations and cafes on country roads—dogs, rab
   ducks, and Dutchboys
several potatoes
galvanized tin bucket
paring knife
newspaper

## COSTUME PLOT

MATTIE

gray Thirties waitress' outfit
black shoes
seamed hose

RONNIE

gray Thirties waitress' outfit
black shoes
seamed hose

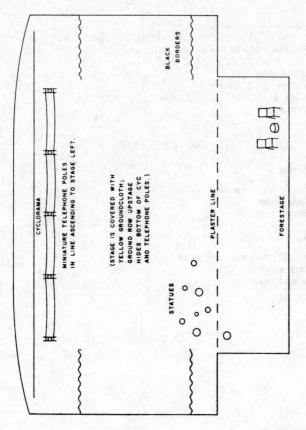

CYCLORAMA

MINIATURE TELEPHONE POLES
IN LINE ASCENDING TO STAGE LEFT.

(STAGE IS COVERED WITH
YELLOW GROUNDCLOTH;
GROUND ROW UPSTAGE
HIDES BOTTOM OF CYC
AND TELEPHONE POLES.)

BLACK
BORDERS

STATUES

PLASTER LINE

FORESTAGE

COMANCHE CAFE

# Domino Courts

By *William Hauptman*

DOMINO COURTS was originally performed by the Second Company of the Williamstown Theatre Festival in August, 1975; produced by Nikos Psacharpoulos; under the direction of Barnet Kellman; with the following cast:

| | |
|---|---|
| FLOYD | *Jay Sanders* |
| RONNIE | *Linda Varvel* |
| ROY | *Josh Clark* |
| FLO | *Diane Patterson* |

DOMINO COURTS was first produced professionally by Wynn Handman and Julia Miles at the American Place Theatre in New York in December, 1975; under the direction of Barnet Kellman; with the following cast:

| | |
|---|---|
| FLOYD | *Guy Boyd* |
| RONNIE | *Mary-Elaine Monti* |
| ROY | *Conard Fowkes* |
| FLO | *Regina Baff* |

This production was based on the original set and lighting designs by Rich Eisbrouch; costume designs by Carol Oditz; Production Stage Manager, Andrea Naier.

DOMINO COURTS was subsequently produced by
Wynn Handman and Julia Miles at the American
Place Theatre in November, 1976; under the direction
of Barnet Kellman; with the following cast:

FLOYD ........................ *Guy Boyd*

RONNIE .................... *Jane Galloway*

ROY ..................... *Conard Fowkes*

FLO ........................ *Regina Baff*

Set design by Henry Millman; lighting design by
Eddie Greenberg; costumes by Carol Oditz; production
stage manager, Richard S. Viola.

PLACE: a tourist court in Southern Oklahoma

TIME: an afternoon in August, 1939

## SET DESCRIPTION

The interior of a tourist cabin in the Oklahoma Dust Bowl, 1939. A hot yellow room without realistic detail. On the backwall are a window and a screendoor; but the window has no glass and the screendoor no mesh. Through them can be seen the black horizon of a bare backstage. On the wall is a green fish on a brown plaque. Most of the rest is painted on.

There is bed D. S. L. There is a vanity table D. S. R. There is a standing lamp by the vanity and a standing coatrack by the door. U. C. is an enclosed kitchen with a pass-through and a row of shelves opening onto the room. In the kitchen is an opening to another, unseen room. There is a folded cardtable and four folding chairs, one by the vanity, two on either side of the pass-through, and one sitting on the rug in the center of the room. In the foreground, on end tables, are two black china cats.

## AUTHOR'S NOTE

*DOMINO COURTS* was inspired by several things: by the prose of Edward Anderson's *Thieves Like Us*, a forgotten Depression novel that's had two movie versions; by a reunion with some of my oldest friends in a cabin outside of Uvalde, Texas, in 1971; and by a shoebox of old photographs my parents kept in the closet, where I found unfocused sepia-tone snapshots of them standing in front of a car in Tulsa, Oklahoma, in 1939—a brown decade with soft outlines, a time before I was born. It does not take place in the real Oklahoma, nor is it about the real Depression. My hometown is only ten miles south of the Oklahoma border, and as a child in the early Fifties I can remember dust storms that blew so thickly they had to turn on the streetlights at noon. *DOMINO COURTS* takes place in my imagination; and Oklahoma, because of its physical relation to my hometown, has always been a dusty landscape without realistic detail hanging somewhere above my head.

# Domino Courts

*Preshow music is heard. The Mills Brothers singing
\*"Paper Doll." As the song plays, the houselights dim;
as it ends the houselights go dark and the stage goes
black.*

*Noon.* FLOYD *sitting on the bed, wearing a suit, holding his hat in his hand. His jacket is on the coatrack. Another, identical hat sits on chair in the
center of the room. When the stage brightens,*
FLOYD *speaks:*

FLOYD. The Hot Grease Boys, that's what they used
to call us. We thought we were hot grease. You should
have seen us in those days, walking in a bank and
sticking our guns in their faces and saying hand over
your money. Hot Grease. That was before Roy and I
split up. When I close my eyes, I can still see us driving down the highway, the centerline disappearing
under the hood. I can see us driving at night, headlights
shining in our faces and those silver posts going by
along the sides of the road. Then they found out who
we were. You started seeing our pictures everywhere—
in the papers, in the post office. Oklahoma was getting
too hot for us; so I retired and Roy drove North.
(*Crossing to chair where hat sits.*) Wait up, Roy, I
shouted, you forgot your hat. But the car was already
moving and he couldn't hear me and I watched him
vanish in a cloud of dust. That was four years ago.
Now Roy's coming back, and I can see the look on his
face when I show him I've still got his good hat.
(FLOYD'S *wife,* RONNIE, *enters. She wears a bathrobe
over a bathing suit. She sits at the vanity, ignoring*

FLOYD, *and starts brushing her hair, looking in the mirror.* FLOYD *doesn't look at her.*) I remember the day we busted that bank in Mound City. I remember us on the road. I remember that last hot day, the car moving and me shouting and the car gone. Dust on my good shoes. Hot—hot—oh, we thought we were so hot . . . (*Pause.*)

RONNIE. Talking to yourself again, Floyd?

FLOYD. I get worked up. They'll be here soon.

RONNIE. I don't know why they couldn't come to our house in town.

FLOYD. It's private out here in the country. Nobody knows our faces out here, we can do what we want.

RONNIE. Nobody knows us in town either.

FLOYD. (*Crossing suddenly to window.*) There's a car coming.

RONNIE. It's not them.

FLOYD. It's not slowing down . . . it's gone past. How'd you know?

RONNIE. I always know what's going to happen. Sit down, Floyd, they're not coming yet. (FLOYD *sits in chair by window and continues to stare out.*) You should go for a swim.

FLOYD. Not me. I'm not going to be standing around without any clothes on when Roy comes. Nosir. (*Pause.*)

RONNIE. I think you're jealous of Roy. He's still working. You'd like to be famous again.

FLOYD. No. No, he's not that famous now. You never see his name in the papers anymore, not now that we've split up. But when we were together, nobody could stop us. (*Crossing back to the hat on the chair.*) I hope you brought your gun along, Roy. We could still show them. What a character you were, you old pisspot. I always said if we were a deck of cards, you'd be the joker. I'm talking about Roy. That's his hat. (*He puts it on, leaving his own hat on the chair.*) How do I look?

RONNIE. It looks like your hat.

FLOYD. But this is Roy's hat . . . (*He advances toward her menacingly.*)

RONNIE. Let's play dominos.

(FLOYD *stops instantly; turns and starts unfolding the cardtable. When he starts talking again, he talks like a hoodlum.*)

FLOYD. She likes to play dominos. Do you? I've always thought it was a waste of time myself. Cards— that's my game. And bingo. I do like the way the dominos look. There's several versions of dominos. One's called forty-two and another's called moon, and that's how I got to know you, Roy. Yeah. (*He works silently for a moment.* RONNIE *ignores him. He moves the chair with his hat left in front of bed and positions the cardtable* C. S.) Good old Roy. We both had the same dream when we were boys, didn't we? That's how close we were. We dreamed about the Man in the Moon. I always thought I looked like him. When I was a boy I used to lie awake nights and watch him floating there, outside the window, thinking we both had the same ghostly grin. So does Fred Astaire. Those are the only other people I've ever wanted to be. Good old Roy. We burned up the roads in those days, didn't we? (*Normal voice, crossing to window.*) There's another car coming—

RONNIE. It's not them. Sit down, Floyd. (*He sits, instantly.* RONNIE *drags her chair from the vanity to the table, sits* U. C. *and starts setting up a row of dominos.* FLOYD *joins her, bringing the chair he was sitting in and placing it* S. L. *He drags it very slowly so it scrapes the floor.*)

FLOYD. That scare you? That loud noise?

RONNIE. No.

FLOYD. (*Sitting; sadly.*) I used to scare you when we were first married. That's the trouble, I don't now.

RONNIE. This is making you nervous, isn't it?

FLOYD. What?

RONNIE. Seeing Roy again.

FLOYD. Why should I be nervous? You're the one
who should be nervous. You're going to be meeting his
new wife, comparing yourself to her. (*Pause.*) I just
hope he brought his gun along. That scare you?

RONNIE. It's your move. (*He tips over a row of
dominos. She starts setting up another one.*)

FLOYD. Why should I be nervous?

RONNIE. It's been four years. People change.

FLOYD. Not Roy. Some people would, but not him.
(*Standing, getting excited.*) That's what was so important about the day we stuck up the Mound City
Bank. Roy was disguised as Clark Gable. We always
did our jobs disguised as movie stars. He'd drawn a
little moustache on his face with a pencil; he said he
only wished his ears stuck out more. I was disguised
as Fred Astaire. I had on my patent leather shoes and
my trousers with the black satin stripe. When he
asked me who I was, and I told him, he said that was
all wrong: Clark Gable and Fred Astaire never made
a movie together yet, and anyway, who ever heard of
a dancing stickup team? Then he looked at me, and he
rubbed off that pencilled moustache. Let it go, Floyd,
he said. Hell—let's be ourselves. So he shook my hand
and I stopped grinning and we busted that bank as
the Oklahoma Hot Grease Boys, and it went for over
four thousand dollars. (*Almost like a boy.*) There's
another car coming, can I go look?

RONNIE. You could never go back on the road again,
Floyd. Not now.

FLOYD. You talk about me as if there was something
wrong with me. I'm not old.

RONNIE. I didn't say you were old.

FLOYD. (*Agitated.*) There's nothing wrong with me,
Ronnie. Why . . . you talk about me as if I was an

alcoholic! (*Laughs loudly.*) Maybe I do want to join up with Roy again. Maybe he feels the same way. Maybe I brought something along that would make your blood run cold.

RONNIE. (*Bored.*) Did you bring your gun?

FLOYD. That's for me to know and you to find out. (ROY *appears behind them in the door.* RONNIE *sees him over* FLOYD'S *shoulder, gasps and points.* ROY *is dark-haired, handsome, sleek, and looks apprehensive. He wears a suit almost identical to* FLOYD'S *and carries two yellow suitcases like a porter.*) Roy . . . (ROY *says nothing. He just grins.*) You old pisspot. (ROY *starts out.*) Roy—it's me—Floyd! Don't you know me? This is my wife, Ronnie. (FLOYD *starts toward him.* ROY *abruptly motions no. He cases the cabin first, disappearing into the kitchen.* FLOYD *gets his jacket from the coatrack and puts it on,* RONNIE *straightens her robe.* ROY *reappears, every move alert, and manhandles the suitcases* D. S. R., *taking a long time, looking around the room. When he speaks, it is almost in a whisper.*)

ROY. Everything looks so small now. So small and flat . . .

FLOYD. You don't look any different, Roy!

ROY. The buildings are so much larger up North. That must be it. But driving down here, things get smaller and smaller. The road changes. Goes from a turnpike to a blacktop to that narrow little dirt road outside. When you finally get here, Oklahoma's no bigger than a tablecloth. . . . Your house looks like a doll house, Floyd. Look at that chair! (*He points and laughs.* FLOYD *laughs, then catches* ROY'S *eye and stops abruptly.*) Like to introduce my wife, Flo. Flo! (*He crosses and shouts out the door. Nobody appears.*)

FLOYD. (*Starting towards them.*) Those suitcases look heavy—

ROY. (*Crossing quickly back to suitcases.*) There's

nothing in them. Nothing but Flo's things and some hotel towels. I can't stop stealing them . . . (*Pause.*)

RONNIE. Can we see her? (FLO's *face appears at the door. She is drab and timid.*)

FLOYD. (*Booming.*) Well, come on in, honey, and let us have a look at you! (FLO *disappears again.*)

RONNIE. Floyd, not so loud. (FLO *reappears.*) I'm Ronnie.

(*She holds out her arms.* FLO *steps hesitantly into the cabin, first removing her hat and wiping her feet. She hands* RONNIE *flowers. Then they suddenly embrace.* FLOYD *backslaps* ROY, *and* RONNIE *takes the flowers into the kitchen.*)

FLOYD. This is something! Boy, it's good to see you, Roy!

ROY. Same here.

FLOYD. Hey! You remember the invisible rope? (*They leap apart* D. S., *stand facing each other.*) We stand on either side of the road. A car comes along and— (*They pull an imaginary rope taut between them.* FLO *gasps.*) Can you see it?

FLO. It looks real.

FLOYD. He slams on his brakes, and when he gets out we make him give us all the money he's got. Go on— try to cross it.

FLO. (*She puts her hands over her eyes and runs through it.*) Oooh.

FLOYD. Go on, Ronnie. Can't you almost feel it?

RONNIE. (*Crossing slowly to rope, smiling.*) Yes.

FLOYD. (*Scornfully.*) You can't feel it, there's nothing there. (*He embraces* ROY. RONNIE *clears dominos from cardtable and sets tablecloth and four plates while* FLO *wanders.*) Boy, this is gonna be great. We'll stay up all night talking about the days of the Hot Grease Boys, the Mound City Bank, the old invisible rope trick, and our dream about the moon.

Roy. . . . Dream about the moon?

Floyd. Sure, you know. Our dream.

Roy. We had a lot of trouble finding this place. (*Looking around, easing somewhat.*) I think you gave us the wrong directions, Floyd. Maybe not. I didn't dream the town would look so small now. We almost didn't find it at all. . . . Just four houses. That's not much of a town.

Floyd. You're not in town, Roy. This is a tourist court.

Roy. No wonder we had so much trouble finding it. Why'd you do that?

Ronnie. Who knows? Floyd wanted to rent a cabin for some reason.

Floyd. So we could do what we wanted. (*Booming.*) So we could make as much noise as we wanted.

Roy. (*Crossing to* Ronnie *at table.*) Floyd wrote me lots about you. I don't know how he got such a good-looking woman.

Floyd. (*Bringing the remaining chair* D. S. *and trying to get between them.*) You haven't changed, Roy. Not a particle.

Roy. Neither have you, Horseface.

Floyd. So tell us about things, about things up North.

Roy. For one thing, I'm thinking about joining a mob.

Flo. (*Picking up a shrivelled balloon off end table* D. R. *and putting it in her purse.*) Somebody had a party . . . (*The others ignore her.*)

Floyd. A mob?

Ronnie. He means a gangster mob, Floyd, like in the movies.

Floyd. I know that; sounds good.

Ronnie. Floyd. Not so loud.

Floyd. I might like to get in on that action. Think one of those mobs would consider taking on another country boy?

RONNIE. You don't look right, Floyd. Not for that. (*To* ROY.) You are handsome. You've got a profile like the magician in the comic strips. You'd look exactly like him if your hair was blue.

FLOYD. I'll show you your cot.

ROY. (*He stiffens again, grabs suitcases.*) I don't think so, Floyd. Flo and I have got to go straight back. We're just passing through this part of the country.

FLOYD. But . . . We were going to talk. There's a pond in the back so we can swim and I was going to cook us a big supper. You've got to stay.

ROY. (*Starting toward the door.*) I've got important things cooking up there, Floyd. (FLO *is standing still, looking out the window.*) What are you looking for?

FLO. A chair. So I can . . . sit down. (*She crosses slowly down to the table, looking at* ROY, *selects the* U. C. *chair and sits.*)

RONNIE. (*Breaking the silence.*) Stay as long as you can. I'm dying to hear about things up North.

ROY. All right. But just for a while.

(ROY, RONNIE, *and* FLO *sit around the table;* RONNIE S. R., ROY S. L. FLOYD *doesn't sit, but remains standing* U. S. R., *staring at* ROY. ROY *sits on* FLOYD'S *hat.*)

RONNIE. Now. I want to hear about the clothes, and Floyd will want to know all about the new model cars.

ROY. I'll make it short. You can get anything you want up North. But you've got to think clear. When I first got there, I was confused. I don't know if I can describe it, but . . . To make a long story short, I found the right people; started hanging around the right places. In fact, I've got my own nightclub now. The Panama Club.

RONNIE. It sounds glamorous.

Roy. You should see it. You wouldn't know it if you did. It's shaped like a jungle. I hired a colored band and there's palm trees and all the waiters wear gorilla suits. Nothing up there is what it seems. It's a whole new world. You can be anyone you want. To make a long story short, I've finally found the place where I belong . . . (*Pause.*) Floyd? You going to join us? (FLOYD *sits in the chair to* FLO's *left, never taking his eyes off* ROY.) So as soon as I join the mob, I'm on my way to the top. I can't say too much more about it, but . . . my head's clear and I've got both feet on the ground. And I'm not coming back to Oklahoma again, because everything's fine now except the old things look small . . . (*Looking around uneasily.*) Everywhere I go, everything looks smaller now than I thought it should . . . I guess because now my mind is so large . . . (*He finishes, staring at* FLOYD.) You're looking good, Floyd. (FLOYD *doesn't answer. Everyone looks at the tabletop.*) Floyd? What are your plans? (*As he says "plans,"* FLO *coughs so the word is inaudible.*)

FLOYD. What?
Roy. Your plans.
FLOYD. Ronnie? What are my plans?
RONNIE. He hasn't got any.

(*As she says "hasn't got any,"* FLO *coughs so the words are inaudible. Each time she coughs, they glance at her momentarily.*)

Roy. What?
RONNIE. He hasn't got any. (*Pause.*)
FLO. There's a lot of dust in the air down here.
Roy. (*Sharply.*) That's not polite, Flo. (*Pause.*) You wrote me a postcard saying you had some plans.
FLOYD. I was going to start a cafe. Ronnie's a good cook— (*As he talks in a low voice,* FLO *coughs and*

*continues coughing so he is almost inaudible.*) We thought we might start a short-order place. You know . . . blue-plate special . . . home-made pies . . . and . . . all that. Ronnie's a good cook. But . . . we gave it up.

ROY. So you don't have any plans? (FLOYD *nods his head "yes".*) Yes you do or yes you don't? (FLOYD *shakes his head "no".*) You don't? (FLOYD *shakes his head "no."*) I give up, it's impossible to have a conversation with you. Say what you're trying to say.

FLOYD. You're sitting on my hat.

ROY. Oh. (*He removes the crumpled hat from underneath him and tosses it on the bed. He stands, crosses around the table to* FLOYD.) You've got to understand, Floyd, the things we did in the old days . . . that was small potatoes. Shotguns and small town banks. That was small potatoes. So you never started a cafe and you don't have any plans. I'm disappointed in you, Floyd. Can't you do anything? (FLOYD *suddenly stands and jerks the tablecloth towards him. The dishes clatter to the floor. Silence. They all stare at him.*)

FLOYD. I thought I could pull it out from under the plates . . . Sorry. I'm all right.

ROY. (*Watching* FLOYD *as he clumsily starts restoring tablecloth and plates.*) Sure. You've just been down here in the Dust Bowl too long, Floyd. (*He slaps him on the shoulder. Dust flies out of* FLOYD'S *suit. He doesn't see.* ROY *and* RONNIE *laugh.*)

FLOYD. What's so funny?

ROY. Nothing.

FLOYD. Am I doing something wrong?

ROY. No. Nosir. (*He slaps him again, more dust.* ROY *covers his mouth with his hand.*)

RONNIE. (*Standing.*) Why don't you go for a swim, Floyd?

ROY. Why don't you? Cool off. Flo can go with you,

and I'll sit here for a while and get to know your wife.

FLOYD. That sounds like a good idea. (*He goes to the door, takes off jacket and leaves it on the coat-rack.*)

ROY. Flo? (*She joins* FLOYD *at the door without a word. They start out.* FLOYD *stops and turns.*)

FLOYD. You won't be gone when I get back, will you?

FLO. I'm your hostage. Roy couldn't leave without me, could he? (*She bats her eyes. They exit.* RONNIE *and* ROY *are standing facing each other across the table. Silence.*)

ROY. How low you sunk. I don't believe it. Does he know?

RONNIE. No.

ROY. Four years . . . I wouldn't have thought he was your type.

RONNIE. (*Smoothing tablecloth nervously.*) He's not the man he was.

ROY. So I noticed.

RONNIE. He's got some kind of problem. I think he drinks.

ROY. He didn't drink before.

RONNIE. Well, something's wrong with him.

ROY. That's obvious.

RONNIE. Maybe you could help him out. I'd think so much of you, if you could light a fire under him.

ROY. (*Draws back suddenly.*) Please! Don't say that.

RONNIE. Why not?

ROY. Just don't. (*Smugly.*) You should have come with me. You wanted me, but you were afraid of me. So I guess you settled for Floyd out of disappointment.

RONNIE. I never wanted you.

ROY. What do you do now?

RONNIE. Play dominos.

ROY. What a waste. (*As he speaks,* RONNIE *picks up the plates and puts them in the kitchen. Then she crosses to the vanity, picks up a Flit gun and walks around the room slowly, spraying.*) I remember the first time I saw you. I walked in the Comanche Cafe and there you were, looking great in your white uniform. It was thin as paper so I could almost see through it and you had a pencil stuck behind your ear. And you said, "May I take your order?" (*Grabbing her* D. L.) You don't fool me. You're Floyd's wife now, but you'd still like to take orders from me, wouldn't you?

RONNIE. Do you really have a nightclub?

ROY. Hell, yes. (*He lets her go, walks* U. S. C.) You should see it. A real night spot.

RONNIE. It sounds magic. I wish I could. Before, when I knew you, I always thought something magic was going to happen to me. I had premonitions, thought I could foretell the future. Sometimes I still think I can. I believed in ghosts.

ROY. Yeah.

RONNIE. I thought there was more to the world than just what you can see. I believed someday a ghost story would happen to me. But I never saw one. And I married Floyd, and now I play dominos. (*She walks around the room spraying again.*)

ROY. Did you have a premonition I was coming?

RONNIE. Yes.

ROY. You know why I left Oklahoma, doll?

RONNIE. You were running from the law.

ROY. They could never have caught me. No, I'd gotten too smart for this place. Didn't I tell you ghost stories were a lot of baloney? Nobody believes in ghosts—not if they're smart. And I was the brains of the Hot Grease Boys. (*She walks away, spraying.*) Come back here!

RONNIE. I'm nervous.

ROY. Stand still when I'm talking to you! (RONNIE *freezes.*) You've still got a good figure. Still dream of being in the movies? (*She smiles, drops Flit gun on bed. She removes her robe, straightens her shoulders so her breasts rise, and walks across the room* S. R., *almost in a trance, the robe flung over her shoulder. Then she catches herself and stops.*) Miss! (*She freezes.* ROY *sits at the cardtable like a customer. She approaches him like a waitress.*)

RONNIE. Could I take your order?

ROY. That's more like it. (*Leaning back in chair.*) I know a lot of things you don't. I'm smart. (*Pulling her down on his lap.*) You see those flies on the ceiling? How do you think they do it?

RONNIE. What?

ROY. Walk on the ceiling. Wouldn't you like to know how?

RONNIE. (*Uncomfortably; trying to get up.*) I shouldn't have left the windows open.

ROY. But wouldn't you like to know? Why do you think they can do it and we can't?

RONNIE. Because they're smart?

ROY. (*Grabbing her angrily now, trying to kiss her.*) Forget Floyd. Come back up North with me—

RONNIE. What about your wife?

ROY. Forget Flo. Look at me—

RONNIE. No! (*She slaps him. He throws her roughly to the floor.*)

ROY. (*Dramatically.*) Hell, you don't know what you're missing. I could show you sights you never dreamed of. Picture it: you and me headed North, driving through the night. There's a star hanging over the end of the road, and I point the car at it. I'm driving faster and faster, the closer we get, and I'm telling you things that make your mouth water. Just us and the billboards going past in the dark, and the stars . . . I could show you a star that's shining so hard it sweats . . . (ROY *has found the snaps on his suitcase. It springs open.*)

RONNIE. What's that? (*He pulls out a black tuxedo.*)

ROY. That's my soup and fish—for the Panama Club.

RONNIE. You must look handsome in it. Let me see you wearing it.

ROY. (*Crossing to her.*) I might do it, doll—if you'll be nice to me. (*Their faces are almost touching.*) You have on bright red lipstick . . . (*They kiss.* FLOYD *appears in the doorway. His hair is sopping wet. He has on bathing trunks, his shirt, shoes, and socks, and there is an unlit cigar jammed in his mouth. He takes them in. Their mouths stay glued together. He comes* D. S., *sits in chair left of table, and speaks loudly.*)

FLOYD. Oh, boy. You should try that pond. Boy, do I feel good now. (ROY *and* RONNIE *have broken apart.* FLO *appears in the door.*) That's all I can say. That was a wonderful experience. Soaking in that nice warm pond water . . . I soaked all my troubles out.

FLO. Can we go swimming?

ROY. No.

FLO. I watched Floyd. It looked like fun.

FLOYD. (*He strikes a kitchen match, holds it to his cigar.*) Sure you don't want to try it, Roy?

ROY. Please. Don't hold that match so close to that table. It could go up in flames, it's only cardboard! (*He lunges forward and blows it out. Everyone stares at him.*) Look at Floyd's socks. (*They are fallen down in* FLOYD'S *shoes. He points and laughs.*)

FLOYD. (*Blowing out a cloud of smoke.*) You don't know what you're missing until you've soaked in that nice warm pond water. You should both go . . . soak yourselves.

ROY. We're going—

RONNIE. Please stay! It seems like you just got here.

FLO. I'm so hungry I could eat a horse!

FLOYD. Then sit right down, honey. We wouldn't dream of letting you go until you've had your supper.

Ronnie? Set the table. (*He pulls back a chair for her. She sits:* RONNIE *starts restoring the plates and table-cloth.*)

FLO. Thank God.

FLOYD. Nosir. You deserve to eat at least.

FLO. I didn't want to be impolite, but I was so hungry I thought I was going to faint.

RONNIE. You look sort of pale, honey.

FLO. You don't know. A minute ago when I was standing out there in that hot sun, I thought, Flo, you're going to faint.

FLOYD. No danger of that now, honey. Soup's on. You want a stogie?

FLO. No.

FLOYD. You can have anything you want here, don't be afraid to speak up.

ROY. I'm staying-but only if Floyd will talk about this situation man-to-man. Will you? (FLOYD *nods.*) Can you be serious about it?

FLOYD. If you want to.

ROY. You know what I'm talking about? (FLOYD *nods.*) Then let's get down to it.

FLOYD. Fine; let's talk about it. (ROY *sits.*)

ROY. You're willing?

FLOYD. It's fine with me, I think it's about time we did.

ROY. All right. Let's get to the point. Ronnie says there's something wrong with you. You've got a serious problem. (*Looking at* RONNIE *and* FLO.) Now I've known Floyd here for a long time, and he's a great guy. But I have noticed this one flaw in Floyd, it's that he—where you going? (FLOYD *has crossed and sat on the bed.*)

FLOYD. You looked at her, I thought you were talking to her. (*Pause.*)

FLO. We gonna eat now? (*No one answers.*) Roy's never told me about you and Ronnie. He never talks about his past; he's always talking about his plans, or the mob. I guess he wanted Oklahoma to surprise me. But now that I met you, I like you. (*To* RONNIE.) I'll bet Floyd's a good cook.

ROY. Flo.

FLO. I don't know how to cook. Neither does Roy. We're always saying we're going to learn, but we never have time, we're always on the go.

ROY. Flo.

FLO. I met Roy at the movies.

RONNIE. Sounds romantic.

FLO. He was sitting on the balcony with his feet propped on the seat in front of him. I knew you shouldn't do that. I guess I'm trying to say he had an air of danger about him. I was ushering, so I shone my flashlight in his face and asked him to please stop. He looked so handsome. He asked me to sit down and share his popcorn with him, and I couldn't believe anyone like him would be interested in me—he was so handsome, and I'm so plain. (*Pause.*)

FLOYD. (*Pointing at a cloud of cigar smoke.*) I saw a cloud outside. Now there's one inside. (*Not looking at* ROY.) You goin' for a dip, Roy?

ROY. Not now.

FLOYD. You don't like the water, do you, Roy? You're like a cat.

FLO. Maybe we could all go for a dip . . . after we've had lunch.

ROY. No.

FLO. But I want to go, Roy. I want to go for a dip.

ROY. No dip.

FLO. My throat's getting dry again. How about it? We can have a nice home-cooked meal, then the four of us can go for a dip—

ROY. Shut up, Flo!

FLOYD. Don't treat her that way.

ROY. I'm trying to help you solve your problem.

FLOYD. What about your problem? (ROY *stiffens, stands.*) Shoe's on the other foot now, isn't it? You know what I'm talking about. At least I haven't changed my personality. You're playing a part. Flo doesn't know because she didn't know you before, but you've got another personality now. (ROY *goes to* FLOYD, *grabs the cigar out of his mouth, breaks it and drops it on the floor.*)

ROY. What's it like?

FLOYD. What?

ROY. This so-called phony personality.

FLOYD. It's something like a fish.

ROY. Why'd you say that?

FLOYD. (*Staring at the fish on the wall.*) I don't know. That's just how it strikes me.

ROY. You'd better lay off the booze, Floyd; that's all I've got to say.

FLOYD. I am not a drunk!

ROY. Ronnie says you are.

RONNIE. I never caught him at it . . .

ROY. Well, something's wrong with you. You act like you don't know me anymore, you talk like you've lost your mind, and you haven't got any plans.

FLOYD. I planned for us to stay up all night reminiscing about our days on the road and all **our** dreams.

ROY. Don't start that crap again, Floyd. I had **no** such dream about the moon.

FLOYD. You did!

ROY. I did not! (FLO *faints. Her head smashes down on the tabletop.*)

RONNIE. She's fainted.

ROY. (*Trying to revive her.*) Flo—snap out of it, Flo.

FLO. I thought we were going to eat. I had such high hopes . . .

ROY. We haven't got time for that now.

FLO. I like Floyd. Stop bothering him. Floyd's like me, he says things; he just opens his mouth and they come out . . . but not like he meant. I thought that was why you liked me, Roy. I say funny things and I make you laugh. Like the other day when I was tired and I told you my feet were on their last legs.

ROY. Do we have to talk about this? The important thing is Floyd's problem. Hell, Floyd; I saw it coming a long time ago. You never could have made it up there. That's why I wanted to go it alone. You don't know how much nerve it took. (*Crossing* D. S. R.) The first night I stayed in a cheap hotel. I'll never forget looking out the window and seeing the searchlights shining in the sky—a new movie premiere or another filling station opening somewhere. Down below there were guys climbing out of taxicabs with beautiful women wearing furs. Nobody in this city ever sleeps, I thought—nobody who I'd want to know.

RONNIE. It sounds just like I dreamed it would. Wonderful.

ROY. I wanted to stay awake, but I couldn't. I kept staring at the brown wallpaper. The carpet was so moth-eaten you got drowsy just looking at it. There was a green stuffed chair and an empty glass and the lamp shade was full of dead flies. I knew I wouldn't always be staying in cheap hotels like that, but I felt like if I slept I'd be . . . dirty somehow. I thought, Roy, this is not the way to get started. So I did something dangerous to stay alert. I got a box of matches and lay down in bed and lit them one at a time. I knew if I fell asleep while one was burning the bedspread would go up in smoke—hell, the whole hotel would. There's almost nothing that won't burn, you know. Once a fire starts it can get out of control so easy, and that's why . . . (*Faint sound of a fly in the room.* ROY *snatches, catches it in his bare hands.*) You've got to stay alert! Sometimes I thought I heard footsteps in the hall—

probably bellhops. But it sounded like somebody was
looking for me. Don't lose your nerve, I thought. Those
guys in the mobs will be looking for you soon enough.
That's just your Good Angel. Everything took nerve up
there. But if you just stay alert, nothing can go wrong. . .
(*Sound of the fly again. He picks up a flyswatter off the
vanity and crosses back to the table.* FLOYD *looks slightly
confused, his eyes unfocused as if the story has hypnotized
him.*) But you, Floyd, you're drowsy. You live in a dream.
Look at you. (*He smacks the flyswatter down on the table.
Everyone starts.*) It's a hard world out there. They don't
forgive mistakes. Have you forgotten guns, Floyd? (*He
smacks the flyswatter down several more times.*) You've got
to stay awake. But you—you're hiding from the world
down here, living in some kind of a soft dream—because
you're afraid. You've got to pull yourself together! (FLOYD
*snatches the tablecloth out from under the plates. Not one
falls to the floor. He stands there grinning triumphantly.*
FLO *applauds.*)

RONNIE. Why don't you put on your soup and fish?
Show him how good you look when you walk into
your club.

ROY. (*Crossing to suitcases.*) I'm going to show you
how we do things up North, Floyd. Understand? I'm
going to show you how to do things in style. (*He
exits.*)

FLO. Good bread, good meat, good God let's eat. We
going to eat now? No.

FLOYD. Do you think I should let Roy talk to me
that way? (RONNIE *gets up without answering and
goes* D. S. *to the vanity, taking her chair with her; sits
and starts brushing her hair.* FLOYD *looks at* FLO.) You
afraid of Roy? Does he make you nervous? I know,
you can't say anything. (*He takes* ROY's *hat and
places it on the floor* D. S. *Then, while they wait, he
sits in the* S. L. *chair, takes a deck of cards out of his
pocket and pitches them at the hat. Some of them go*

*in.*) I'm Floyd Simms. Roy probably hasn't told you
my name. Four years ago I was as famous as him, but
now . . . That's how it goes. There's no getting along
with him. If you say something he doesn't like, he'll
bite your head off. (FLO *gets up when he says this and
crosses to the bed and sits.*) I understand. Roy thinks
Oklahoma is small potatoes now. He wants to be moving on. Roy's talented, he could always talk to people . . . all sorts of people. I never could. (*Pause.*)
I'm doing something wrong. I know I'm doing something wrong. Seems like nothing's ever important
enough for you, so you let it go. You don't even try.
Then there's all the little things that are always
happening to you that make you sad. You fall asleep
in the afternoon and you don't wake up until the sun's
gone down. There you are in a dark room; you don't
know how you got there, and it makes you sad. Or you
go to a show but you don't get there until the last
feature. At first it's crowded, but then people start
leaving. Finally, you're almost alone. And when the
lights come on you walk up the aisle real slow, looking over your shoulder at the credits, showing you've
got all the time in the world and you're not afraid
to be the last one out of there. It makes you sad. Or
you go to a store to buy clothes. You feel pretty good—
then suddenly here it comes, out of a mirror in the
corner, that face you don't recognize at first because
you've never seen yourself from that angle before.
Then you see it's you and it makes you sad and you
walk out of there without buying any clothes. What
am I talking about? Something about success, I
think . . . Look at my socks. It just makes you sad
the way you let things go, because nothing's ever . . .
important enough for you. Because you're not. I'm
wasting my life. (*To* FLO.) One thing: do you think
I'm handsome?

FLO. You got a sad face. But it's nice. It's like those pictures you see in the drugstore window. They're yellow and faded from being in the sun for so long, and they look sad. But when you look closer, you see they're really movie stars . . . (*They look at each other.* FLOYD *smiles.* ROY *appears, wearing the tuxedo. He walks slowly* D. R. *to* RONNIE; *proud, making the final adjustments—straightening tie and cuffs.*)

ROY. I look great, don't I? Admit it.

RONNIE. (*Standing, circling around him.*) Oh, yes. Those trousers. That boiled shirt. Those shiny black shoes.

ROY. Nothing like being well-dressed and ready to face the world. How do you like it?

RONNIE. Won't you look, Floyd? He's just trying to help you.

ROY. You could look like this if you could lick your problems, Floyd. You know your worst enemy is yourself.

FLOYD. I got something for you, Roy. I forgot to give it to you.

ROY. (*Eagerly.*) A present?

FLOYD. (*Smiling sadly.*) I hid it somewhere in this room.

ROY. Can I have it now?

FLOYD. If you can find it. (ROY *starts looking, under the table, in the vanity. Meanwhile, unnoticed,* FLOYD *takes a black Lone Ranger mask like his from under the bed and places it in the hat he has been pitching cards into. He gives* ROY *directions.*) You're getting warmer. You're getting hot now. Hotter. No—you're cold. (ROY *goes into the kitchen, pokes around the shelves.*) You're getting warm again. (FLOYD *goes to the coatrack and pulls on his pants, ignoring* ROY *as he ransacks the room. He keeps giving him hints.* ROY *searches more and more frantically until he has turned the cabin upside down, getting now hotter and now colder, upsetting the chairs, throwing the covers off the bed, pulling out the vanity drawer and emptying it on the floor. The girls follow him, trying to pick up. When* FLOYD *has gotten his pants on the room is demolished and* ROY *has found the mask.*)

ROY. Hell, Floyd, I'm touched. Where'd you find this? (*He puts it on.*) You know this means a lot to me, don't you, Horseface?

FLOYD. Sure, you old pisspot.

ROY. You know it's hard up there in those big cities—and you've got to be the same way if you want to make it. Maybe I've been too hard on you today.

FLOYD. Nobody liked you up there, did they, Roy?

ROY. What?

FLOYD. That's why you came back—you got lonely.

ROY. You're wrong about that, Floyd.

FLOYD. Be ourselves, you said that day in Mound City. But you're not! You even told me you had the same dream I had, like we were one person.

ROY. You starting that crap again, Floyd?

FLOYD. Something was chasing you in the dark, under the moon. You didn't know what, but you woke up in a cold sweat.

ROY. I don't remember.

FLOYD. You're lying! You've got to!

ROY. I never work up in a cold sweat about anything, (*Putting his arm around* FLOYD *patronizingly.*) Floyd, What's happened to you? It's like you died. There was a time I didn't think you were afraid of anything. Look at you now.

FLOYD. Let go!

ROY. Don't you think two men can touch each other? What's the matter, you afraid of me, too, Floyd? Are you afraid to try?

FLOYD. Let go of me, you jerk! (*He pushes* ROY *away,*

*snatches up flyswatter off the end table.*) Try to screw my wife, will you! (FLO *gasps.*) It's true! I saw them!

my wife, will you! (FLO *gasps.*) It's true! I saw them!

FLO. It's not true, is it, Roy?

ROY. I made a pass at your wife. But she was asking for it.

RONNIE. (*Ashamed.*) He said he wanted me to run away with him, and I believed him. He told me he was going to take me to his nightclub.

ROY. You married a tramp, Floyd. If I'd been around I could have told you. (FLOYD *advances with the flyswatter.*) You've got to get mighty close to use that. (*He swings, ROY jumps him, forces him to let go of it like you would a gun; throws* FLOYD *down.*) I don't scare easy, Floyd.

FLOYD. I didn't scare you with that?

ROY. I don't know the meaning of the word.

FLOYD. (*Pulling gun out of his trouser pocket.*) What about this? Hold still, or I'll blow you apart! You're not the only one who can be a tough guy. This puts us on equal ground, doesn't it?

ROY. Is it loaded?

FLOYD. You want to find out? Ronnie?

RONNIE. You wouldn't shoot, Floyd. Not me.

FLOYD. Oh, wouldn't I? Get over there against that wall, both of you. *Move!* (*They do.* FLOYD *lies down casually on the bed, gun still pointing at them, hat pulled down low over his eyes, and his head propped on one hand.*) Now. I'm gonna lie here and watch you spill your guts. Do you feel like pleading for your life, Roy? Ronnie? Would you plead for him? I've been hearing about up North and I've been hearing about your bigshot nightclub ever since you got here; and now I'm fed up. You're gonna drop this phony personality—or you're gonna die!

FLO. There's no nightclub!

Roy. Flo!

Flo. Don't, Floyd. You're making a mistake, you can't shoot him!

Ronnie. No nightclub?

Roy. She's right. It's gone—burned in a horrible fire. I couldn't tell you. It's the worst thing that ever happened to me. (*Rushing on dramatically.*) I'll never forget the palm trees and tablecloths burning, and the tinsel on the ceiling and the women's hair. The smoke came boiling down so thick you couldn't see or breathe. Flo and I are the only ones who got out alive. She can tell you—how I pulled her into the kitchen and we crawled into the icebox. When the firemen got us out the next morning, there was nothing left but ashes. So go ahead and shoot, Floyd—I've got nothing left to live for now anyway. But do you know why I really came back down here? I wanted to join up with you again. Like in the old days. Look, Floyd, I know you're still sore about your wife. But don't let her come between us. It could be like it was, Floyd—you know, the two of us, driving in the heat. I can almost see it now. You know, those old days were great . . . (*Suddenly he grabs* Ronnie, *holds her in front of him as a human shield.*) OK, drop your gun, Floyd; it's a stalemate! Floyd? (Floyd *doesn't react. He advances cautiously on bed, still holding* Ronnie *in front of him.* Floyd *is asleep.*) You shithead! (*He throws his hat down on the floor and tramples it.*) And that's for your hat!

Ronnie. It's your hat. So—there's no more Panama Club.

Flo. There never was one! You got that from that story you heard about that joint that burned down in Boston, and you're so afraid of fire and all you couldn't stop talking about it. (*She lights a match.*) The Panama Club was another one of your plans. But you'll never do it. You'll never stay in one place long enough to do anything. (*She backs him out the doorway with the match.*)

Roy. I'm going for a walk. To . . . clear my head. (*He exits.* Flo *lights a last match, blows on it, drops it in the ashtray. It doesn't go out. She blows on it and ashes fly all over the table.*)

Flo. Sorry.

Ronnie. Forget it.

Flo. I know: I'm plain. I'm not good-looking like you. But it seems to me I deserve to eat. I'm so bored with always being on the move. But I'm afraid I'll lose him. Then when Floyd said that about you and Roy . . .

Ronnie. Yeah.

Flo. You're not to blame. I can't keep him interested. I thought I could, but . . . something's always bursting my balloon.

Ronnie. Let's wake up Floyd.

Flo. Why?

Ronnie. He'll know what to do. (*They go and stand over him.*) Floyd? (*He doesn't move.*)

Flo. Rise and shine, Floyd.

Ronnie. He's out like a light. It's getting dark outside. Another day almost gone. You've got to learn how to deal with men. You know how to dance?

Flo. No—

Ronnie. I'll show you. (*She turns on the radio. They do a brisk two-step to "I Found a Dream" by Bob Wills.* Ronnie *keeps stepping on* Flo's *feet.*)

Flo. You were a waitress?

Ronnie. Yeah.

Flo. That's been my problem—restaurants. He likes to eat out, you know. Travel and eat out. Always moving.

Ronnie. Things are gonna look up for you soon, honey.

Flo. You think so?

RONNIE. I know so. You're a good kid. (FLO *gives up. Turns off radio.*)

FLO. Look . . . maybe you could teach me how to play dominos. (RONNIE *gets dominos, turns on lamp and they sit. By now, the room is quite dark.*) See, it's not the food in restaurants I can't deal with. It's the menu. You've got to order your food by the name on the menu or they won't bring it to you. So if you ask for breakfast, they say, don't you mean the Little Red Hen? You want a steak and they say, Oh, you mean the Panhandle T-Bone Platter. You want to cover your head with the tablecloth, but you've got to say it out loud. It goes worse and worse. Bring me your Pittsburger. Bring me your Tater Tots. If there's a number, you can say, Bring me the Number Four, thank God. But mostly it's bring me the Chew N' Sip, bring me the Thanksgiving Turkey in the Straw. Bring me a Bromo, I'm sick. There must be more to life.

RONNIE. (*Knocking over a row of dominos.*) Yeah.

FLO. A blue-plate special—that's what I ask for. Anyone can say they want the blue-plate Special. You've heard it asked for in the movies. So they bring it, and I eat it even if it's something I don't like. The thing is, it never is anything I like. What I really wanted was a blue plate. By now, it's the only thing I'm hungry for. A nice, blue plate. I want the food I hear them eating on the radio—it sounds so good when they talk with their mouths full. I want the food they eat in movies, the food mice eat in cartoons. I wish I was in a cartoon. (*Voice breaking.*) Somebody would hit me on the head and stars would fly out . . .

RONNIE. Don't you think you could talk him into settling down?

FLO. I can give you the answer to that in two words? Im possible.

RONNIE. Don't cry honey, no man's worth it. (ROY *rushes back in. He stops just inside the door, his back pressed to the wall. He has no pants.*)

ROY. Don't go out there! There's something out there. Something loose in the bushes. (*Looks down.*) Where's my pants? Flo, go back and get my pants.

FLO. Where are they?

ROY. I know: I left them on a branch. It was a dog— a big dog loose in the bushes. Flo, go out and get my pants. (*She laughs.*) That's an order.

FLO. I can't take him seriously. I never knew your legs were so white.

ROY. Somebody's got to. My keys are in them. Flo?

FLO. Why don't you get them yourself if you want them so bad?

ROY. I was down by the pond. For some reason I thought I'd like to go wading, so I took off my trousers so they wouldn't get wet. There was mud and dead leaves on the bottom. The water was cold. I was wishing I had a light so I could see if there were any fish, and then whatever it was must have heard me; because something came rushing towards me through the woods— an animal on the loose! I thought it might be a dog—a mad dog. So I lit out before it could catch me and bite me; lit out so fast I forgot my pants. I ran so hard I felt like I was floating. The moon was shining down the whole time with this cold grin, like it had nothing to do with me. And it was like it had all happened to me before. Like a dream...or a nightmare I had when I was a kid...and tried to forget.

RONNIE. You sound scared.

ROY. Hell, no—I'm not scared. But how can I walk around here without any pants on?

RONNIE. Pretend you're at a nudist camp.

ROY. But we've got to go. We've got to start back up North. Hit the road.

FLO. We can start tomorrow. Sit down, let's play dominos; Ronnie's showing me how.

ROY. (*Crossing to* RONNIE.) You'll get them for me,

won't you?

RONNIE. You're making this whole thing up so we'll feel sorry for you, aren't you?

ROY. No! There's something out there.

RONNIE. You'll wake Floyd.

ROY. I tell you, the dog is real.

RONNIE. Like your nightclub? (*She picks up Flit gun and advances on him.*) Why'd you ever have to come back here?

ROY. Ronnie— (*She sprays him in the face.*)

RONNIE. Siddown! (ROY *hesitates. She pulls back the handle of the Flit gun threateningly; he crosses quickly and sits in the* S. R. *chair.* RONNIE *then sits in the center chair.*) Now. We've got the whole night ahead of us. Let's tell ghost stories.

FLO. Oh, good. I like being scared.

RONNIE. Let's turn out the lights so it'll be spookier.

FLO. Roy? Turn out the lamp. (*He looks at her uncertainly.*) Come on, honey, be polite.

ROY. She can turn it out herself.

FLO. You're closest.

ROY. (*He gets up, goes to the lamp and stops.*) What happens if I do and that dog comes in? (*He goes to the kitchen and gets a rolling pin.*) I'll use this to protect myself. (*He crosses back to the lamp.*) Here goes.

FLO. Nothing's going to happen, honey. (*He turns off the lamp.* FLOYD *groans, startling* ROY, *and sits up in bed.*)

FLOYD. Unnnh....(*He looks at* ROY.) You still here?

ROY. (*Starting toward him.*) Floyd, it's been swell, but we've got to go—

FLO. Come and sit down, honey. I'm not going anywhere.

ROY. I guess . . . we'll stay instead. (*He goes back and sits at the table holding his rolling pin. The girls are playing dominos. Without lamplight the stage is bathed in a melancholy bluish glow.*)

RONNIE. I haven't told ghost stories since I met Floyd. But it seems like tonight ghost stories might be possible. There's one about a drowned girl. That was one of my favorites. (*Standing, taking position U. C. to create the mood.*) You're driving by the lake one night and her ghost stops you. She's got wet hair and she asks you in a real sad voice, Can I have a ride home? You don't know she's a ghost yet. So you say, yeah, and for some reason she gets in the back seat and you start back to town. You're nervous, and you keep trying to see her in the mirror, because all the way you think you can feel her eyes staring at the back of your head. But when you get to her house, it's gone. (*She stops, thinks hard.*) Or it's a haunted house. No.

FLO. Her parents come out and tell you their daughter drowned four years ago.

RONNIE. Yeah.

FLO. I heard that one before. I didn't want to spoil your story.

RONNIE. It was my favorite one. I used to know thousands of ghost stories. Thousands. Now I'm not sure I can remember how any of them end. But wasn't it frightening? Floyd?

FLOYD. How come the lights are out? (*He gets up, goes to the lamp. But instead of turning it on, he notices* ROY *and stops.*) You're half nude, Roy. What for? (*He goes to the kitchen and comes back a moment later with a steak on a plate. He puts it on the table in front of* ROY *and stands, waiting.* ROY *looks at everyone. He prods the steak with a fork. It squeaks and he draws back, startled, dropping the fork. He looks up; everyone is smirking at him. Then he puts his head down on the table and begins to sob quietly. Coldly.*) OK, Roy. You got the part. (FLOYD *crosses to the coatrack, puts on jacket, takes a cigar out of the pocket and puts in in his mouth.*)

FLO. You tell one now, Floyd. I want to hear a real one—about ghosts wearing sheets, with holes for eyes. Haunted houses. About somebody waiting for you by the side of the road,a hitchhiker who glows in the dark.

FLOYD. (*Sitting at table between the girls.*) In the old days, Roy and I drove through all those small dark towns at midnight. Not a light burning. And you'd read the signs out loud. You couldn't stop yourself. City Limits. Spark Garage. Utopia Hardware Store. Gas. Cactus Cafe. Airport Motel. Sunset Motel. Gas. Then you were out in the dark again, moving on.

RONNIE. Where does the ghost come in?

FLOYD. Nobody saw you. You felt like a ghost.

ROY. ...You felt like you were dead. There was nothing to go back to, and nothing ahead but more empty towns like that. So you kept moving. How did I end up back here in Oklahoma? It's the last place I wanted to be. There must be somewhere left to go! (*Suddenly he stands.*) There's something under the bed!

FLO. I don't hear anything.

ROY. Listen! (*They do, turning out front. Nothing is heard.*) Have you got that dog under there, Floyd?

FLOYD. I think you've lost your mind, Roy. I don't have a dog.

ROY. You don't? Don't fool me.

FLOYD. Look for yourself. (*Pause.*)

FLO. Let's sing to keep our spirits up. (*Pause. Nobody sings. Nobody looks at anybody else.* RONNIE *stops playing dominos. When* ROY *starts singing, she begins again.*)

ROY. I'm gonna buy a paper doll that I can call my own . . and not a . . . (*He falters and stops. They all look at him. When he starts singing again, they go back to playing dominos.*) I'd rather have a paper doll . . . that I could call my own . . . (*Silence.*)

That doesn't sound like me. I'd never have a paper doll.

FLOYD. Like I say, that's your problem. (*He gets up, moves around the table and takes* ROY's *chair.*) Gimme a light, Flo. (FLO *strikes a match and holds it to his cigar.*)

ROY. I think I'd better have a look under that bed.

FLOYD. You still nervous, Roy? I'll look for you.

ROY. No. I'll do it.

FLOYD. Suit yourself. (ROY *goes over and starts crawling under the bed,* U. S.)

RONNIE. Sometimes you wonder where it's all gone. I know now I'll never leave Oklahoma. And Floyd and I will never start a cafe. My ghost story was a failure and I don't think I'll have anymore premonitions now. I can't even remember why ghosts should scare you . . . something about the word boo. I'm sticking to dominos. They don't surprise you, but who needs surprises? Dominos is fine from now on. Except for sometimes you think you should walk out the back door and drown yourself in that pond . . .

FLOYD. (*Standing and crossing up to the door, looking out and smoking.*) I liked that pond. I was lying on my back, looking up at floating clouds. It felt like I was floating up there in the sky with them . . .

ROY. (*Under bed.*) Floyd?

FLOYD. Roy?

ROY. There's nothing under here. You were right. But a while ago I could have sworn you had a vicious dog around here you weren't telling me about.

FLOYD. There's no dog.

ROY. Good. But if there was, you wouldn't let him in here, would you?

FLOYD. Nope.

ROY. Good. (*Pause.*) But I think I'll stay under here for a while anyway. Things look pretty good under here. I'm going back up North tomorrow. I'm going

alone—as Clark Gable. You know, you're all in a
fog. That's what's wrong with you. Your minds aren't
clear, like mine. But things look fine under here. And
I'm leaving first thing tomorrow. (*Pause.*) As soon as
Floyd calls off his dog.

RONNIE. In the old days, when I worked at the
Comanche Cafe, everything was special. What went
wrong?

FLOYD. Wind. That wind started blowing and overnight
this country turned into the Dust Bowl. Everything died.
Nothing could grow. Nobody had any money. (*Coming
back down to sit* S.R. *at the table.*) But worse than that, you
couldn't think for blowing dust. There was nothing more to
do, and it seemed like everyone was killing time, waiting
around and coughing, and everything sounded dead, like it
does on a record when the music's over and there's nothing
to hear but the empty part, just scratches going round...
and round...

FLO. I like it here. I'm never leaving this place again.
(*She takes the balloon out of her purse and starts to
blow it up.*)

FLOYD. One thing was good—driving. When you were
moving down the road, in the heat; and somewhere
way out in front of you, you could see that water
shining on the road. Those silver puddles where the
centerline hits the horizon. They always made me so
mad. I drove faster, trying to get there before they
dried up. I drove slower, trying to keep them in sight.
But before you got there, they were always gone. They
were the best thing—and they weren't even real.

FLO. (*Showing him the balloon.*) Look, Floyd. (*He
grins. They grin at each other, and he pops it with
his cigar. Silence.*)

FLOYD. Only the sound of our guns was real. (*The
stage is bathed in a bluish glow.* FLOYD *is looking out,
puffing his cigar.* RONNIE *and* FLO *are bent over the*

*table,* ROY *hidden under the bed. The air is cloudy with smoke. In the distance, a dog barks. The stage darkens slowly.)*

# DESCRIPTION OF PLAY

The time: 1939, the end of the Depression. Somewhere in the Dust Bowl of Southern Oklahoma, in one of the cabins of the Domino Tourist Courts, two couples have a strange reunion. The men, FLOYD and ROY, are the former Hot Grease Boys, a bank stick-up team who haven't seen each other for four years. FLOYD has stayed in Oklahoma, gone straight and tried to start a cafe. ROY has journeyed North to join one of the big-city mobs. FLOYD has married RONNIE, an Oklahoma waitress; and ROY has married a movie usher he met up North named FLO. From the moment they see each other, the changes they've undergone are obvious. FLOYD has become confused and depressed and may be an alcoholic. ROY is so nervous he sees every object in the room as a potential menace. When FLOYD and FLO go outside for a swim, ROY and RONNIE are left alone: we find out that they spent a night together four years ago, but FLOYD doesn't even know they've met. RONNIE begs ROY to help FLOYD with his drinking problem—if that is what's wrong with him. ROY tells her he owns his own nightclub now, the Panama Club, and asks her to leave FLOYD and return North with him. They kiss—FLOYD appears in the door, coming back from the pond, and sees them. When the four sit down to resolve things the truth comes out about what ROY has really done up North. In the last part of the play, as evening draws on, the couples are left isolated by darkness and the unreality of the arid landscape all around them. Their illusions are gone; nothing is what they thought it was. Each one is alone,—trapped by unreachable ambitions, nostalgia, boredom, and fear. At times, *Dominio Courts* becomes surreal, almost a magic show, as the chills underneath the comedy come to the surface, and books, cigars, tablecloths, and banal phrases all take on a life of their own.

# CHARACTER DESCRIPTIONS

FLOYD—ROY calls him Horseface. About thirty; homely, awkward and confused; but with a warm, slow grin and a sensitive nature. He may have a drinking problem. He idolizes ROY and lives in the past, the days of the Hot Grease Boys. Aware at times that his good-looking wife, RONNIE, is a little too much for him.

RONNIE—Vain but sensible underneath; ultimately loyal to FLOYD. She's a combination of sensuality and common sense, and formerly a waitress. She, too, is living in the past, on the memory of her night with ROY. Loves stories of the supernatural. Believes she sometimes has the power to foretell the future. Wanted to be a movie star but never went to Hollywood.

ROY—Handsome, energetic, older than FLOYD, and a liar. He has a sharp, dry voice and may affect gangster mannerisms. At times appears lost and disoriented. Underneath is full of tremendous anxiety; taut as a steel wire. He desires solitude but can't stand it when he gets it.

FLO—Drab and timid, was a movie usher. ROY is the only man she's ever had. May speak with Northern accent. FLO is perpetually hungry but can't stand restaurant food; is perpetually starved for reality.

## PROPERTY LIST

1 twin bed with 2 white sheets, 2 pillows in white pillowcases, and a bedspread
2 small end tables
2 black china cats
a window shade
a kitchen curtain
Thirties radio
small vase
plain water glass
heavy white china plates with simple borders
silverware wrapped in cloth napkins
4 folding cardtable chairs
1 folding cardtable
large oval braided rug
standing coatrack
standing lamp with shade (practical)
a vanity table with drawer and mirror
green fish on a brown plaque
artificial flowers (for Flo to bring)
plain white towel
El Producto cigars
large balloons (at least 10″ diameter)
1 black Lone Ranger mask
2 yellow suitcases with brown bands
assorted make-up on vanity: lipstick, nail polish, Kleenex, nail file, brush, hair pins, curling iron
deck of cards
rolling pin
rubber steak on a plate with fork and knife (can be found at the supermarket as squeeking dog toy)
hand gun
dominos in a box
tablecloth (light cloth easier to pull out from under plates)
small glass ashtray; large glass ashtray
strike anywhere wooden matches
dummy tuxedo inside suitcase
small box matches

hat (identical to FLOYD's *and* ROY's)
Flit gun
flyswatter

(Obviously several of some of these items will have to be purchased.)

## PRODUCTION NOTES

"Paper Doll" and post-show music ("I'll be Around") can both be found on THE MILLS BROTHERS GREATEST HITS album (see Cautionary Note, p. 26).

The actor will find it easy to jerk the tablecloth out from under the dishes if he jerks it *down,* not straight toward him. This is an old trick, and much simpler than it looks.

# COSTUME PLOT

**FLOYD**
  light-weight grayish brown suit
  white shirt
  suspenders
  tie (loud)
  brown socks
  brown wing-tip shoes
  handkerchief
  gray bathing suit with sailboat pattern
  white t-shirt
  wide-brimmed hat


**RONNIE**
  hot pink floor-length satin robe
  two-piece brown, white, and pink bathing suit
  pink platform pumps
  ankle bracelet
  pink hair ribbon


**ROY**
  light-weight brownish-beige suit
  suspenders
  white shirt
  tie
  brown socks
  two-tone brown and beige wing-tip shoes
  bright colored jockey shorts
  wide-brimmed hat
  white handkerchief
  black tuxedo with dress shirt
  cufflinks
  black bow tie
  black patent leather shoes

FLO

  faded pastel print dress
seamed stockings
yellow hat and purse
umbrella
brown low-heeled shoes
sweater
pearl necklace and bracelet

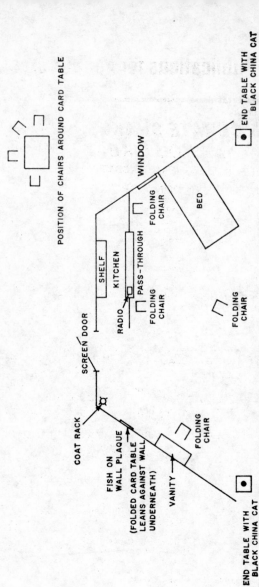

POSITION OF CHAIRS AROUND CARD TABLE

END TABLE WITH BLACK CHINA CAT

WINDOW

BED

FOLDING CHAIR

SHELF

KITCHEN

PASS-THROUGH

RADIO

FOLDING CHAIR

FOLDING CHAIR

SCREEN DOOR

COAT RACK

FISH ON WALL PLAQUE

(FOLDED CARD TABLE LEANS AGAINST WALL UNDERNEATH)

VANITY

FOLDING CHAIR

END TABLE WITH BLACK CHINA CAT

**DOMINO COURTS**
GROUND PLAN AT OPENING CURTAIN

# Other Publications for Your Interest

---

## THE CURATE SHAKESPEARE
## AS YOU LIKE IT
### (LITTLE THEATRE—COMEDY)

### By DON NIGRO

#### 4 men, 3 women—Bare stage

This extremely unusual and original piece is subtitled: "The record of one company's attempt to perform the play by William Shakespeare". When the very prolific Mr. Nigro was asked by a professional theatre company to adapt *As You Like It* so that it could be performed by a company of seven he, of course, came up with a completely original play about a rag-tag group of players comprised of only seven actors led by a dotty old curate who nonetheless must present Shakespeare's play; and the dramatic interest, as well as the comedy, is in their hilarious attempts to impersonate all of Shakespeare's multitude of characters. The play has had numerous productions nationwide, all of which have come about through word of mouth. We are very pleased to make this "underground comic classic" widely available to theatre groups who like their comedy wide open and theatrical.  (#5742)

---

## SEASCAPE WITH SHARKS
## AND DANCER
### (LITTLE THEATRE—DRAMA)

### By DON NIGRO

#### 1 man, 1 woman—Interior

This is a fine new play by an author of great talent and promise. We are very glad to be introducing Mr. Nigro's work to a wide audience with *Seascape With Sharks and Dancer*, which comes directly from a sold-out, critically acclaimed production at the world-famous Oregon Shakespeare Festival. The play is set in a beach bungalow. The young man who lives there has pulled a lost young woman from the ocean. Soon, she finds herself trapped in his life and torn between her need to come to rest somewhere and her certainty that all human relationships turn eventually into nightmares. The struggle between his tolerant and gently ironic approach to life and her strategy of suspicion and attack becomes a kind of war about love and creation which neither can afford to lose. In other words; this is quite an offbeat, wonderful love story. We would like to point out that the play also contains a wealth of excellent **monologue** and **scene material.**  (#21060)

# Other Publications for Your Interest

## *HUSBANDRY*
### (LITTLE THEATRE—DRAMA)

### By PATRICK TOVATT

#### 2 men, 2 women—Interior

At its recent world premiere at the famed Actors Theatre of Louisville, this enticing new drama moved an audience of theatre professionals up off their seats and on to their feet to cheer. Mr. Tovatt has given us an insightful drama about what is happening to the small, family farm in America—and what this means for the future of the country. The scene is a farmhouse whose owners are on the verge of losing their farm. They are visited by their son and his wife, who live "only" eight hours' drive away. The son has a good job in the city, and his wife does, too. The son, Harry, is really put on the horns of a dilemma when he realizes that he is his folks' only hope. The old man can't go it alone anymore—and he needs his son. Pulling at him from the other side is his wife, who does not want to leave her job and uproot her family to become a farm wife. *Husbandry*, then, is ultimately about what it means to be a *husband*—both in the farm and in the family sense. *Variety* praised the "delicacy of Tovatt's dialogue", and called the play "a literate exploration of family responsibilities in a mobile society." Said *Time*: "The play simmers so gently for so long, as each potential confrontation is deflected with Chekhovian shrugs and silences, that when it boils into hostility it sears the audience." (#10169)

## *CLARA'S PLAY*
### (LITTLE THEATRE—DRAMA)

### By JOHN OLIVE

#### 3 men, 1 woman—Exterior

Clara, an aging spinster, lives alone in a remote farmhouse. She is the last surviving member of one of the area's most prominent families. It is summer, 1915. Enter an immigrant, feisty soul named Sverre looking for a few days' work before moving on. But Clara's farm needs more than just a few days' work, and Sverre stays on to help Clara fix up and run the farm. It soon becomes clear unscrupulous local businessmen are bilking Clara out of money and hope to gain control of her property. Sverre agrees to stay on to help Clara keep her family's property. "A story of determination, loyalty. It has more than a measure of love, of resignation, of humor and loyalty."—Chicago Sun-Times. "A playwright of unusual sensitivity in delineating character and exploring human relationships." —Chicago Tribune. "Gracefully-written, with a real sense of place."—Village Voice. A recent success both at Chicago's fine Wisdom Bridge Theatre and at the Great American Play Festival of the world-reknowned Actors Theatre of Louisville; and, on tour, starring Jean Stapleton. (#5076)

# Other Publications for Your Interest

## *THE SQUARE ROOT OF LOVE*
### (ALL GROUPS—FOUR COMEDIES)

### By DANIEL MELTZER

#### 1 man, 1 woman—4 Simple Interiors

This full-length evening portrays four preludes to love—from youth to old age, from inno-
cence to maturity. Best when played by a single actor and actress. **The Square Root of
Love.** Two genius-level college students discover that Man (or Woman) does not live by
intellectual pursuits alone . . . **A Good Time for a Change.** Our couple are now a suc-
cessful executive and her handsome young male secretary. He has decided it's time for a
change, and so has she . . . **The Battling Brinkmires.** George and Marsha Brinkmire, a
middle-aged couple, have come to Haiti to get a "quickie" divorce. This one has a surprise
ending . . . **Waiting For To Go.** We are on a jet waiting to take off for Florida. He's a retired plumbing contractor who thinks his life is over—she's a recent widow returning to
her home in Hallandale. The play, and the evening, ends with a beginning . . . A success
at off-off Broadway's Hunter Playwrights. Requires only minimal settings.          (#21314)

## *SNOW LEOPARDS*
### (LITTLE THEATRE—COMIC DRAMA)

### By MARTIN JONES

#### 2 women—Exterior

This haunting little gem of a play was a recent crowd-pleaser Off Off Broadway in New
York City, produced by the fine StageArts Theatre Co. Set in Lincoln Park Zoo in Chicago
in front of the snow leopards' pen, the play tells the story of two sisters from rural West
Virginia. When we first meet Sally, she has run away from home to find her big sister Claire
June, whose life Up North she has imagined to be filled with all the promise and hopes so
lacking Down Home. Turns out, life in the Big City ain't all Sally and C.J. thought it would
be: but Sally is going to stay anyway, and try to make her way. "Affecting and carefully
crafted . . . a moving piece of work."—New York City Tribune. *Actresses take note*: this
play is a treasure trove of scene and monologue material. *Producers take note*: the play
may be staged simply and inexpensively.                    (#21245)

# Other Publications for Your Interest

## *PRECIOUS SONS*
### (LITTLE THEATRE—COMIC DRAMA)

### By GEORGE FURTH

#### 3 men, 2 women—Interior

This finely wrought new play is a real rarity these days: an original play, originally produced on Broadway. Ed Harris and Judith Ivey starred in this autobiographical drama about a family struggling to make it economically in the late 1940's in Chicago. The father, Fred Small, has a chance for a promotion, which would necessitate the family move to another city. The youngest precious son, Freddy (really the central character), is caught between his desire to be a professional actor and his father's determination that he finish high school and go on to college. Set against everyone is the mother, Bea, who has her own ideas about how the family should be run. "This seemingly innocuous play turns out to contain an emotional force that approaches terror. It's the terror that comes when we realize we don't really know 'the truth'. Is Bea the monster she seems . . . Is Fred an insensitive hulk who deserves to have his dreams trampled by a wife he's unwittingly repressed? Where does love fit into all this—who really loves whom, and how do they love?"—Newsweek. "Furth creates convincing people: he gives them clever, well-wrought and wholly plausible dialogue; and he appreciates the timeless give-and-take of family life, its perilous candor and its resilience."—Time. "Furth has written wonderfully real characters. And given us a play about real things. Honest emotions. Couched in comedy."—WABC-TV. "Powerfully personal . . . A powerful family play . . . has an authentic, gripping dramatic logic that makes its climax seem surprising but inevitable."—Newsweek.                                                                    (#18159)

## *SO LONG ON LONELY STREET*
### (LITTLE THEATRE—COMIC DRAMA)

### By SANDRA DEER

#### 3 men, 3 women—Interior

Audiences and critics alike cheered this excellent new play by a talented new American playwright both in its premiere production by Atlanta's Alliance Theatre and in its pre-Broadway tryout. It also had a short but respectable Broadway run. Set in a rundown old southern house situated on 25 acres of valuable land, the play is about the gathering of the Vaughnum family for the reading of crochety old Aunt Pearl's will. The secrets of three generations of the family are revealed slowly as the current generation tries to decide who is the rightful owner of the property. "A richly-textured work about a disputed inheritance, miscegenation, unrequited incestuous love and greed masquerading as Christian righteousness. Sounds heavy and sensational, but *Lonely Street* is neither. It's a funny and poignant human comedy . . . Southern gothic with a sense of humor and lots of heart."—Variety. "This play would tear the house down *anywhere*. It's just plain wonderful."—Atlanta Journal. "A winner."—Boston Globe. "Zesty, poignant and fiercely funny."—Time Mag.                                                                    (#21254)